A TRUE BOOK™

Physical Science

Matter

ANN O. SQUIRE

Children's Press®
An Imprint of Scholastic Inc.

Content Consultant
Valarie Akerson, PhD, Professor of Science Education
Department of Curriculum and Instruction
Indiana University Bloomington, Bloomington, Indiana

Library of Congress Cataloging-in-Publication Data
Names: Squire, Ann, author.
Title: Matter / by Ann O. Squire.
Other titles: True book.
Description: New York, NY : Children's Press, [2019] | Series: A true book |
    Includes bibliographical references and index.
Identifiers: LCCN 2018034487| ISBN 9780531131411 (library binding) | ISBN
    9780531136041 (pbk.)
Subjects: LCSH: Matter—Juvenile literature. | Matter—Properties—Juvenile
    literature. | Atoms—Juvenile literature.
Classification: LCC QC173.16 .S68 2019 | DDC 530.4—dc23
LC record available at https://lccn.loc.gov/2018034487

All rights reserved. Published in 2019 by Children's Press, an imprint of Scholastic Inc.
Printed in North Mankato, MN, USA 113

SCHOLASTIC, CHILDREN'S PRESS, A TRUE BOOK™, and associated logos are trademarks and/or
registered trademarks of Scholastic Inc.

Scholastic Inc., 557 Broadway, New York, NY 10012

1 2 3 4 5 6 7 8 9 10 R 28 27 26 25 24 23 22 21 20 19

**Front cover: A child looking at a
substance through a magnifying glass**

**Back cover: A child with helium-filled
balloons floating over water**

Find the Truth!

Everything you are about to read is true *except* for one of the sentences on this page.

Which one is **TRUE**?

T or F Gases are not matter because they do not take up space.

T or F Atoms can be broken down into even smaller particles.

Find the answers in this book.

Contents

THE BIG TRUTH!

The Periodic Table

3 Molecules, Elements, and Compounds

Ice

4

Hot-air balloons

1

H

Hydrogen

Hydrogen is the first
element listed on
the periodic table.

Think About It!

Take a look at the photo on these pages. What do you see in the image? Can you find a solid? A liquid? A gas? Do these substances have anything in common? How are they different? Once you have some predictions about *what* you see, think about what made each object what it is.

Intrigued?
Want to know more? Turn the page!

Think about the iceberg, the ocean water, and the clouds in the sky. All of them are made up of water. As we'll learn in the next chapter, water—along with everything else in the world—is a type of matter.

Below are examples of water as a solid, liquid, and gas that you might see in your daily life.

Gas

Liquid

Solid

Geysers such as Old Faithful (shown here) in Wyoming spew hot water, steam, and other substances when they erupt.

But as you can tell by looking at them, these substances are also different! Water and many other types of matter can exist in different forms: solid, liquid, and gas. They are called states. Ice is *solid* water. The ocean water is a *liquid*. The clouds show that the air contains water vapor. This is water in the form of a *gas*.

When raindrops fall to the ground, they splash and flow like any other liquid would.

Precipitation can fall as a liquid—such as rain—or solid—such as snow.

CHAPTER 1

What Is Matter?

Matter can seem like a confusing scientific term. But in some ways, it's very simple. Matter is just stuff. It is your desk at school, the students and teachers in your classroom, the rain outside, and the air you breathe. Everything that surrounds you, and even you yourself, is matter.

Volume and Mass

All matter must have two qualities, or characteristics. First, it must take up space. That's easy to see with many objects. Cars, chairs, and people are solid things that take up space. Oceans, lakes, and rivers are liquids, but they take up space too. Even air takes up space. You can see this when you blow up a balloon. The more air you add, the bigger the balloon grows. The amount of space an object takes up is called its **volume**.

Hot gases allow hot-air balloons to fly.

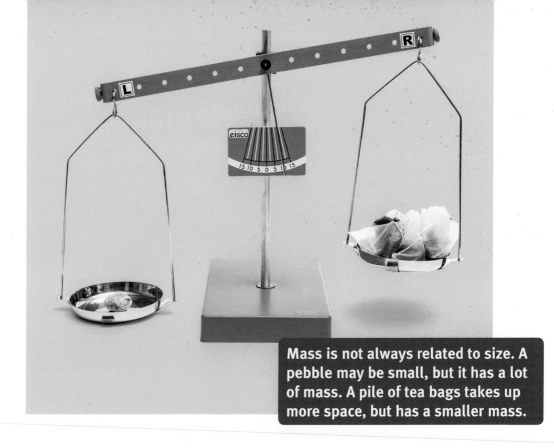

Mass is not always related to size. A pebble may be small, but it has a lot of mass. A pile of tea bags takes up more space, but has a smaller mass.

The second quality of matter is that it has **mass**. This is a measure of how much matter is in an object. To understand mass, it can help to consider a rule about matter. If matter is moving, it tends to keep moving. If it is not moving, it tends to stay at rest. It takes effort to put matter into motion or to stop that motion. The greater an object's mass, the more effort it takes to do this.

Our galaxy contains enough atoms to make up an estimated 100 billion or more stars.

In particularly dark areas, you can see the stars and clouds of gas that make up a portion of our galaxy, the Milky Way.

CHAPTER 2

Building the Universe: Atoms

All matter is made up of the same basic building blocks. The **atom** is one example of these important building blocks. Atoms are the smallest piece that an **element** can be broken into without losing the element's characteristics. These tiny particles combine to form everything in the universe, from a small gnat to a giant galaxy.

Tiny Particles

To give you an idea of just how tiny atoms are, consider this. There are approximately 7 octillion atoms in an average human body. That's a 7 followed by 27 zeros, an almost unbelievably huge number. And all those atoms are made up of particles that are even smaller! Three types of particles make up an atom: **protons, neutrons,** and **electrons**.

You are made up entirely of atoms.

Structure of the Atom

To visualize an atom, think about our solar system. At the center is the sun, and the planets all orbit around this central core. Based on studies, scientists think an atom is structured similarly. The center is called the nucleus. It contains protons, which have a positive charge, and neutrons, which have no charge at all. Electrons whirl around the nucleus. These negatively charged particles are attracted to the positive protons. This holds the atom together.

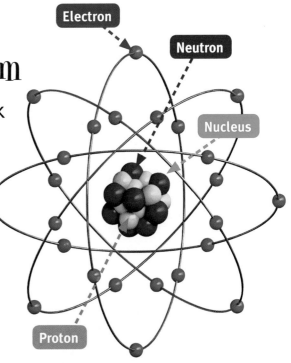

Electron

Neutron

Nucleus

Proton

This is a diagram of a carbon atom. It makes up about 18.5 percent of the human body.

Atomic Number

Atoms are not all the same. Some have more protons, neutrons, and electrons than others. A hydrogen atom has one proton. An atom of gold has 79 protons. Most atoms

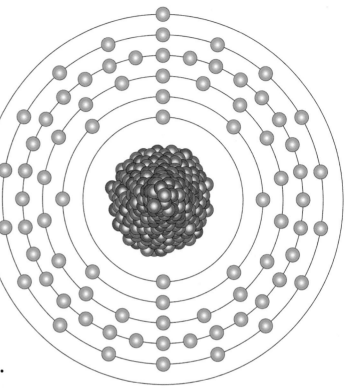

Gold's electrons are spread across several orbits.

have an equal number of electrons and protons. That means a gold atom has 79 electrons whizzing around the nucleus. A hydrogen atom has only one. Scientists have assigned each type of atom an atomic number, based on the number of protons in the nucleus.

Even Smaller!

In the 1960s, physicists found evidence that there are particles even smaller than electrons, protons, and neutrons. These smaller particles, called quarks, make up protons and neutrons. Some scientists predict that we will eventually discover even smaller particles.

Among the particles in an atom, electrons are the smallest. In fact, 1,836 electrons can fit inside one proton! Electrons are part of a family of particles called leptons. Neutrinos, another type of lepton, are produced by the sun and in nuclear reactions. Solar neutrinos can pass through Earth without touching any other particles.

This illustration shows two protons colliding.

The Periodic Table

There are currently 92 known elements that occur naturally. Another 26 elements are made by humans. That makes a total of 118 elements. In the 1860s, Russian chemist Dmitry Mendeleyev created a table called the periodic table. It listed elements in order of their atomic numbers. About 60 elements were known at that time. But as more were discovered, they were added to the periodic table, which is still in use today. As you can see, certain groups of elements share properties.

ATOMIC NUMBER

1
H ← SYMBOL
Hydrogen ← NAME

1
H
Hydrogen

3	4
Li	Be
Lithium	Beryllium

11	12
Na	Mg
Sodium	Magnesium

19	20	21	22	23	24
K	Ca	Sc	Ti	V	Cr
Potassium	Calcium	Scandium	Titanium	Vanadium	Chromium

37	38	39	40	41	42
Rb	Sr	Y	Zr	Nb	Mo
Rubidium	Strontium	Yttrium	Zirconium	Niobium	Molybdenum

55	56		72	73	74
Cs	Ba		Hf	Ta	W
Caesium	Barium		Hafnium	Tantalum	Tungsten

87	88		104	105	106
Fr	Ra		Rf	Db	Sg
Francium	Radium		Rutherfordium	Dubnium	Seaborgium

57	58	59	60
La	Ce	Pr	Nd
Lanthanum	Cerium	Praseodymium	Neodymium

89	90	91	92
Ac	Th	Pa	U
Actinium	Thorium	Protactinium	Uranium

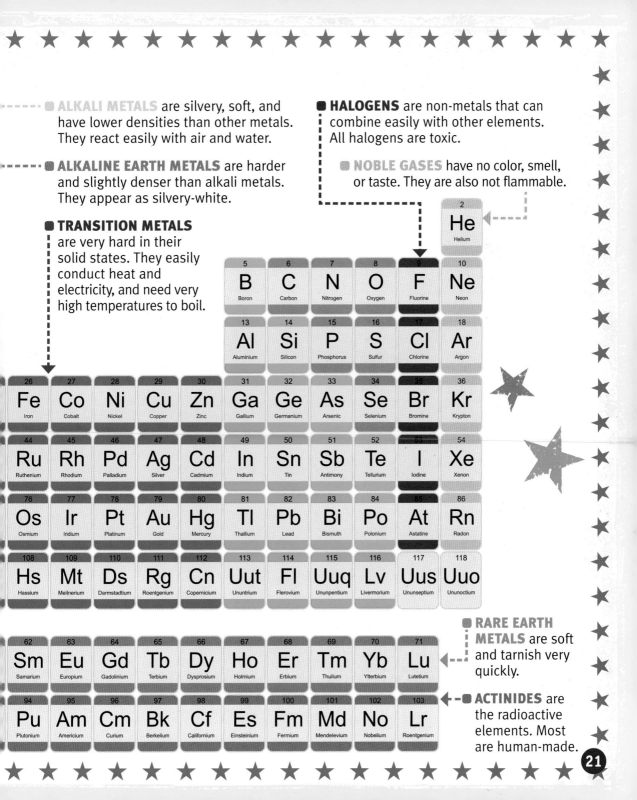

● **ALKALI METALS** are silvery, soft, and have lower densities than other metals. They react easily with air and water.

● **ALKALINE EARTH METALS** are harder and slightly denser than alkali metals. They appear as silvery-white.

● **TRANSITION METALS** are very hard in their solid states. They easily conduct heat and electricity, and need very high temperatures to boil.

● **HALOGENS** are non-metals that can combine easily with other elements. All halogens are toxic.

● **NOBLE GASES** have no color, smell, or taste. They are also not flammable.

● **RARE EARTH METALS** are soft and tarnish very quickly.

● **ACTINIDES** are the radioactive elements. Most are human-made.

| 2 He Helium |

| 5 B Boron | 6 C Carbon | 7 N Nitrogen | 8 O Oxygen | 9 F Fluorine | 10 Ne Neon |

| 13 Al Aluminium | 14 Si Silicon | 15 P Phosphorus | 16 S Sulfur | 17 Cl Chlorine | 18 Ar Argon |

| 26 Fe Iron | 27 Co Cobalt | 28 Ni Nickel | 29 Cu Copper | 30 Zn Zinc | 31 Ga Gallium | 32 Ge Germanium | 33 As Arsenic | 34 Se Selenium | 35 Br Bromine | 36 Kr Krypton |

| 44 Ru Ruthenium | 45 Rh Rhodium | 46 Pd Palladium | 47 Ag Silver | 48 Cd Cadmium | 49 In Indium | 50 Sn Tin | 51 Sb Antimony | 52 Te Tellurium | 53 I Iodine | 54 Xe Xenon |

| 76 Os Osmium | 77 Ir Iridium | 78 Pt Platinum | 79 Au Gold | 80 Hg Mercury | 81 Tl Thallium | 82 Pb Lead | 83 Bi Bismuth | 84 Po Polonium | 85 At Astatine | 86 Rn Radon |

| 108 Hs Hassium | 109 Mt Meitnerium | 110 Ds Darmstadtium | 111 Rg Roentgenium | 112 Cn Copernicium | 113 Uut Ununtrium | 114 Fl Flerovium | 115 Uuq Ununpentium | 116 Lv Livermorium | 117 Uus Ununseptium | 118 Uuo Ununoctium |

| 62 Sm Samarium | 63 Eu Europium | 64 Gd Gadolinium | 65 Tb Terbium | 66 Dy Dysprosium | 67 Ho Holmium | 68 Er Erbium | 69 Tm Thulium | 70 Yb Ytterbium | 71 Lu Lutetium |

| 94 Pu Plutonium | 95 Am Americium | 96 Cm Curium | 97 Bk Berkelium | 98 Cf Californium | 99 Es Einsteinium | 100 Fm Fermium | 101 Md Mendelevium | 102 No Nobelium | 103 Lr Roentgenium |

21

Sand molecules become stickier when mixed with a little water. This allows you to build a sand castle.

One silicon and two oxygen atoms are in every molecule of silica, the most common mineral in sand.

CHAPTER 3

Molecules, Elements, and Compounds

Most matter doesn't consist of isolated atoms. Instead, atoms group together to form **molecules**. When molecules are formed by one single type of atom, the resulting substance is called an element. Gold is a good example. Pure gold consists only of gold atoms. Other elements include silver, lead, oxygen, and hydrogen. Each is composed of one type of atom, and each has a different atomic number.

Compounds

You have probably seen some elements, such as silver, gold, or lead. But if you look around you, most objects aren't made from elements. What are they made of? When atoms of different types group together, the result is a **compound**. Most things we see, hear, touch, taste, and smell every day are compounds.

The smells released by flowers are made up of compounds.

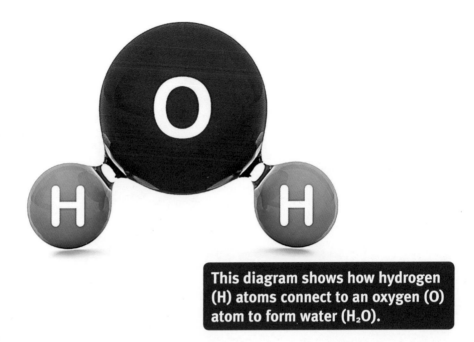

This diagram shows how hydrogen (H) atoms connect to an oxygen (O) atom to form water (H_2O).

There are just over 100 elements, but there are millions of different compounds in the world. They are created when different types, and different numbers, of atoms get together to form molecules. A familiar example of a compound is water. You've probably heard people refer to water as H_2O. That's because every water molecule consists of two hydrogen (H) atoms and one oxygen (O) atom.

Molecular models help students learn how molecules are structured.

Different molecules have different shapes, from lines, to pyramids, to diamonds.

CHAPTER 4

Chemical Bonds

If molecules are made up of multiple atoms, what keeps those atoms together? How do water's two hydrogen atoms and one oxygen atom stick? Why don't the atoms just go their separate ways? The answer is chemical bonds. A chemical bond happens when atoms donate electrons to one another or share them with each other.

Finding Balance

In every atom, electrons circle the nucleus in orbits called shells. Each shell can hold a certain number of electrons. An atom is most stable when its outer shell is full of electrons. Some atoms, however, don't have a full outer shell. This makes the atom unstable. These atoms can find balance in a couple of ways.

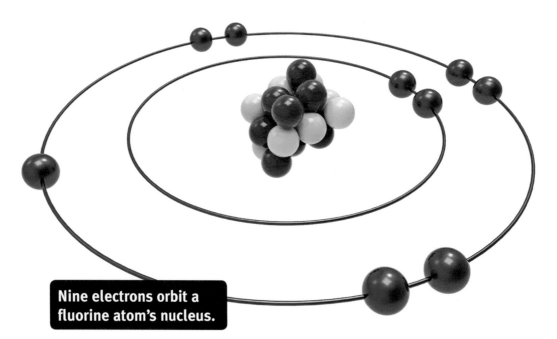

Nine electrons orbit a fluorine atom's nucleus.

Passing Electrons

When one atom passes electrons to another, it forms a molecule with an **ionic bond**. For example, a lithium fluoride molecule has one lithium atom and one fluorine atom. Both atoms are unstable on their own. Lithium's outer shell is almost empty, with one electron. Fluorine has seven electrons in its outer shell,

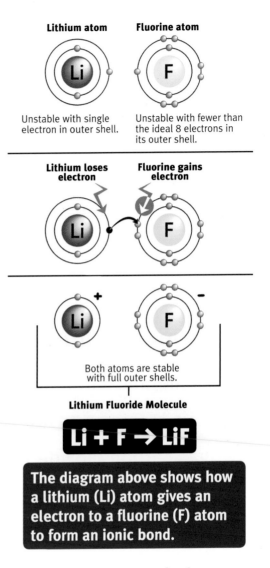

Lithium atom

Unstable with single electron in outer shell.

Fluorine atom

Unstable with fewer than the ideal 8 electrons in its outer shell.

Lithium loses electron

Fluorine gains electron

Both atoms are stable with full outer shells.

Lithium Fluoride Molecule

Li + F → LiF

The diagram above shows how a lithium (Li) atom gives an electron to a fluorine (F) atom to form an ionic bond.

but it needs eight for balance. These atoms can help each other. Lithium transfers its outer electron to fluorine. This rids lithium of its lone outer electron and fills fluorine's outer shell.

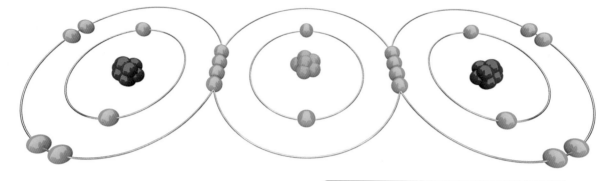

A carbon dioxide (CO_2) molecule has two carbon atoms on opposite sides of an oxygen atom.

Sharing Electrons

Sometimes atoms share electrons with each other. This creates a **covalent bond**. One example is the gas carbon dioxide (CO_2). Each molecule has one carbon and two oxygen atoms. Carbon has four electrons in its outer shell. Oxygen has six. Both need eight electrons for balance. Each oxygen atom shares two electrons with carbon, filling carbon's outer shell. Two carbon electrons are shared with one oxygen atom, and two electrons with the other. This fills the oxygens' outer shells.

Chemical Formulas

As we have seen, we can use abbreviations such as CO_2 or H_2O to represent molecules. These are called formulas. Element symbols (such as O for oxygen) show which elements are present. Numbers indicate how many atoms of each element are in one molecule. For example, cane sugar's formula is $C_{12}H_{22}O_{11}$, with 12 carbon, 22 hydrogen, and 11 oxygen atoms.

Can you figure out what makes up the common compounds below? Look at the periodic table on pages 20–21 to find each element's symbol.

$NaCl$—Table salt (used to season our food)

SiO_2—Sand (found in many deserts and beaches)

NH_3—Ammonia (used as a cleaning product and to help crops grow)

H_2O_2—Hydrogen peroxide (sometimes used to kill disease-causing organisms)

Water is one of the few substances on Earth that can move easily between solid, liquid, and gas.

CHAPTER 5

States of Matter

Everything is composed of matter, but matter can exist in different states. On Earth, most matter appears in one of three states: solid, liquid, or gas. Solids are hard and hold a shape on their own. The atoms are packed tightly together and cannot move around much. The atoms in liquids are farther apart and have weaker connections. The atoms can slide past each other. This is why liquids move around more freely.

Matter Taking Shape

Liquids take up space just as solids do. But liquids take the shape of their container, whether a cup, bottle, or swimming pool.

Gases also take up space. Unlike the tightly packed atoms in a solid, however, those in a gas are far apart, more randomly arranged, and weakly connected. As a result, a gas expands to fill a space.

Timeline of Matter Discoveries

400s BCE
Greek philosopher Democritus argues that objects are composed of smaller building blocks he calls *atomos*.

1897
British physicist J. J. Thomson discovers electrons.

400s BCE ➤ **1789 CE** ➤ **1897**

1789 CE
French chemist Antoine-Laurent Lavoisier writes that even when matter changes its state, its mass stays the same.

Changing States of Matter

Physical events, such as changing temperatures, can change matter from one state to another. Add heat energy to ice, and the solid ice melts to liquid water. Add even more heat energy and the water boils. It turns into a gas—water vapor!

Most substances need extreme energy to change their states.

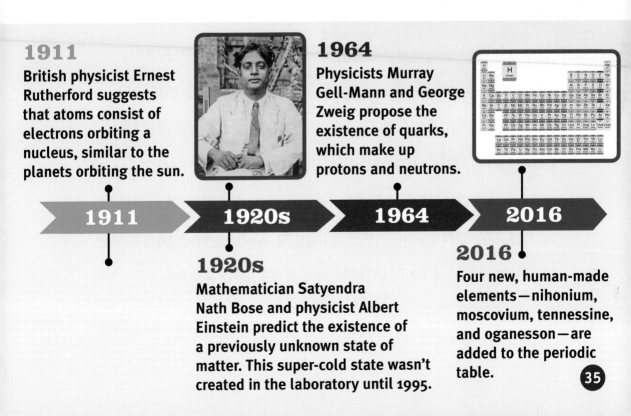

1911
British physicist Ernest Rutherford suggests that atoms consist of electrons orbiting a nucleus, similar to the planets orbiting the sun.

1964
Physicists Murray Gell-Mann and George Zweig propose the existence of quarks, which make up protons and neutrons.

1911 — 1920s — 1964 — 2016

1920s
Mathematician Satyendra Nath Bose and physicist Albert Einstein predict the existence of a previously unknown state of matter. This super-cold state wasn't created in the laboratory until 1995.

2016
Four new, human-made elements—nihonium, moscovium, tennessine, and oganesson—are added to the periodic table.

Propane tank

Propane is a liquid as long as it's inside its pressurized container.

Under Pressure

Increasing or decreasing pressure is another way to make a substance change states. Gas grills burn a fuel called propane (C_3H_8) to cook food. The fuel is kept in a special container. Propane is a gas at normal temperature and pressure. But inside the container, the propane is under high pressure, which forces the molecules closer together. This turns the propane into a liquid. When the propane is released, it immediately turns into a gas.

Matter can sometimes go directly from solid to gas form. This is called sublimation. A good example is dry ice, which is solid carbon dioxide (CO_2). CO_2 has to be very cold to freeze: −109.3 degrees Fahrenheit (−78.5 degrees Celsius) in fact! If it becomes any warmer, dry ice warms and turns into a gas. One important fact is that although the state changes, the matter itself is unchanged. The molecules in dry ice are the same molecules in CO_2 gas.

DESCRIBING PHASE CHANGES

Chemists use specific terms to describe the change from one state of matter to another. Here are some examples.

Chemistry Term	Phase Change
Melt	Solid to Liquid
Freeze	Liquid to Solid
Boil or vaporize	Liquid to Gas
Condense	Gas to Liquid
Sublimate	Solid to Gas
Deposit	Gas to Solid

Chemical Changes

Sometimes, the atomic bonds holding a molecule together break apart. At other times, new atomic bonds form. These events create a new molecule. This is called a chemical change.

Rust is one example of chemical change. When exposed to air, iron (Fe) atoms combine with oxygen (O) atoms. Together, they create iron oxide (Fe_2O_3). We see this new molecule as rust on iron. Other chemical changes include burning wood, a baking cake, and the digestion of food.

Cars rust over time as a result of a chemical reaction between iron and oxygen.

Matter All Around Us

From the tiniest neutrinos to the most massive galaxies, our entire universe is made up of matter. Countless variations of particles and compounds form the food we eat, the stars in the sky, the friends and family around us, and everything in between. And though matter surrounds us, researchers keep learning new information about it. Keep exploring matter, and you may someday make a big discovery yourself! ★

A Simple, Tasty Phase Change Demonstration

Matter can change between states. How?
Investigate using this experiment.

Materials

- ☐ Large pitcher
- ☐ Water (check the juice concentrate can for how much)
- ☐ Can of frozen orange or grape juice concentrate
- ☐ Spoon
- ☐ 5–6 small paper cups
- ☐ 5–6 wooden craft sticks

Directions

1. Add water to the pitcher according to package directions. Open the can of juice concentrate and use the spoon to empty it into the water. Notice the concentrate is frozen and solid. Stir it until the concentrate melts. This is a phase change!

2. Fill each paper cup at least ⅓ full of juice. Place a craft stick into each cup.

3. Place cups into the freezer. Check them after 30 minutes, 1 hour, and 2 hours. What is happening to the juice? Is another phase change occurring?

4. Once the juice is frozen, peel off the paper cups and enjoy. Notice what happens to the juice pops once they are out of the freezer.

Explain It!

Using what you learned in this book, explain what happened to the frozen concentrate and to the cups of juice. If you need help, look back at Chapter 5. And remember, phase changes are reversible!

The Magic Inflating Balloon

How can a gas take up space? This experiment will help you understand.

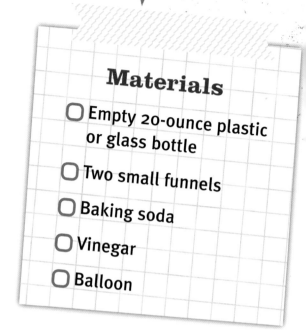

Directions

1. Using one funnel, pour vinegar into the bottle until the bottle is about 1/3 full.

2. Using the other funnel, pour baking soda into the balloon until the balloon is about 1/2 full.

3. Pinch the neck of the balloon to keep the baking soda from pouring out. As you do this, carefully stretch the opening of the balloon over the opening of the bottle.

4. Lift the balloon up and allow the baking soda to pour into the bottle. Watch what happens to the balloon!

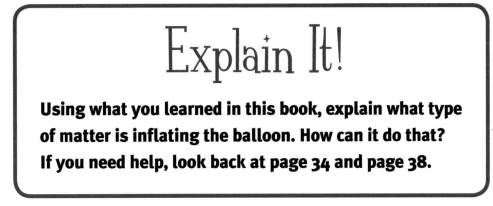

Explain It!

Using what you learned in this book, explain what type of matter is inflating the balloon. How can it do that? If you need help, look back at page 34 and page 38.

Temperature at which water freezes: 32°F (0°C)

Temperature at which water boils: 212°F (100°C)

Number of atoms in one molecule of water (H_2O): 3

Number of atoms in one molecule of carbon dioxide (CO_2): 3

Number of atoms in one molecule of sugar ($C_6H_{12}O_6$): 24

Number of atoms in one molecule of chlorophyll, the substance in plants that absorbs sunlight: 137

Number of electrons that can fit inside a proton: 1,836

Did you find the truth?

F Gases are not matter because they do not take up space.

T Atoms can be broken down into even smaller particles.

Resources

Books

Callery, Sean, and Miranda Smith. *Periodic Table: The Definitive Visual Catalog of the Building Blocks of the Universe.* New York: Scholastic, 2017.

Gray, Theodore. *The Elements: A Visual Exploration of Every Known Atom in the Universe.* New York: Black Dog & Leventhal, 2012.

Slingerland, Janet. *Explore Atoms and Molecules! With 25 Great Projects.* White River Junction, VT: Nomad Press, 2017.

Visit this Scholastic website for more information on matter:
⭐ www.factsfornow.scholastic.com
Enter the keyword **Matter**

Important Words

atom (AT-uhm) the tiny part of an element that has all the properties of that element

compound (KAHM-pound) a substance made from two or more types of atoms

covalent bond (koh-VAY-luhnt BAHND) a connection between atoms in which the atoms share electrons with one another

electrons (ih-LEK-trahnz) tiny, negatively charged particles that move around the nucleus of an atom

element (EL-uh-muhnt) a substance that cannot be divided up into simpler substances

ionic bond (eye-AH-nik BAHND) a connection between atoms in which one atom gives one or more electrons to another

mass (MAS) the amount of physical matter that an object contains

molecules (MAH-luh-kyoolz) bonded combinations of one or more types of atom

neutrons (NOO-trahnz) particles that are found in the nucleus of an atom and have no charge

protons (PROH-tahnz) positively charged particles that are found in the nucleus of an atom

volume (VAHL-yoom) the amount of space taken up by a three-dimensional object or by a substance within a container

Index

Page numbers in **bold** indicate illustrations.

About the Author

Ann O. Squire is a psychologist and an animal behaviorist. Before becoming a writer, she studied the behavior of rats, tropical fish in the Caribbean, and electric fish from central Africa. Her favorite part of being a writer is the chance to learn as much as she can about all sorts of topics. In addition to *Matter*, Dr. Squire has written books about many types of animals, as well as health, earth science, planets, and weather. She lives in Asheville, North Carolina.